Is My Dog a Wolf?

How Your Pet Compares to Its Wild Cousin

Is My Dog a Wolf?

How Your Pet Compares to Its Wild Cousin

Jenni Bidner

LARK BOOKS
A Division of Sterling Publishing Co., Inc.
New York

Editor:
Joe Rhatigan

Art Director:
Robin Gregory

Cover Designers:
Jenni Bidner & Celia Naranjo

Assistant Editors:
Rose McLarney & Carlie Ramer

Art Production Assistant:
Bradley Norris

Editorial Assistance:
Delores Gosnell

This book is dedicated to the wolves of the Wildlife Science Center (Forest Lake, MN) and the dedicated people who care for them.

Library of Congress Cataloging-in-Publication Data

Bidner, Jenni.
  Is my dog a wolf? : how your pet compares to its wild cousin / Jenni Bidner.— 1st ed.
    p. cm.
  Includes index.
  ISBN-13: 978-1-57990-732-7 (hardcover)
  ISBN-10: 1-57990-732-6 (hardcover)
  1. Dogs—Miscellanea. 2. Dogs—Behavior—Miscellanea. I. Title.
SF426.2.B53 2006
636.7—dc22
                                        2005034865

10 9 8 7 6 5 4 3 2 1

First Edition

Published by Lark Books, A Division of
Sterling Publishing Co., Inc., 387 Park Avenue South, New York, N.Y. 10016

© 2006, Jen Bidner

Distributed in Canada by Sterling Publishing,
c/o Canadian Manda Group, 165 Dufferin Street, Toronto, Ontario, Canada M6K 3H6

Distributed in the United Kingdom by GMC Distribution Services,
Castle Place, 166 High Street, Lewes, East Sussex, England BN7 1XU

Distributed in Australia by Capricorn Link (Australia) Pty Ltd., P.O. Box 704, Windsor, NSW 2756 Australia

If you have questions or comments about this book, please contact:
Lark Books, 67 Broadway, Asheville, NC 28801
(828) 253-0467

Manufactured in China

ISBN 13: 978-1-57990-732-7
ISBN 10: 1-57990-732-6

For information about custom editions, special sales, and premium and corporate purchases, please contact Sterling Special Sales Department at 800-805-5489 or specialsales@sterlingpub.com.

Contents

Is There a Wolf in Your House?

This dog wants his owner to throw up. See page 50.

You have just come home from a long day at school, and your dog nearly knocks you over as you put your book bag down. You give him a hug and he starts licking your face. Awww, he loves you. At least that's what you think. But what your dog is really doing is acting like a wild wolf.

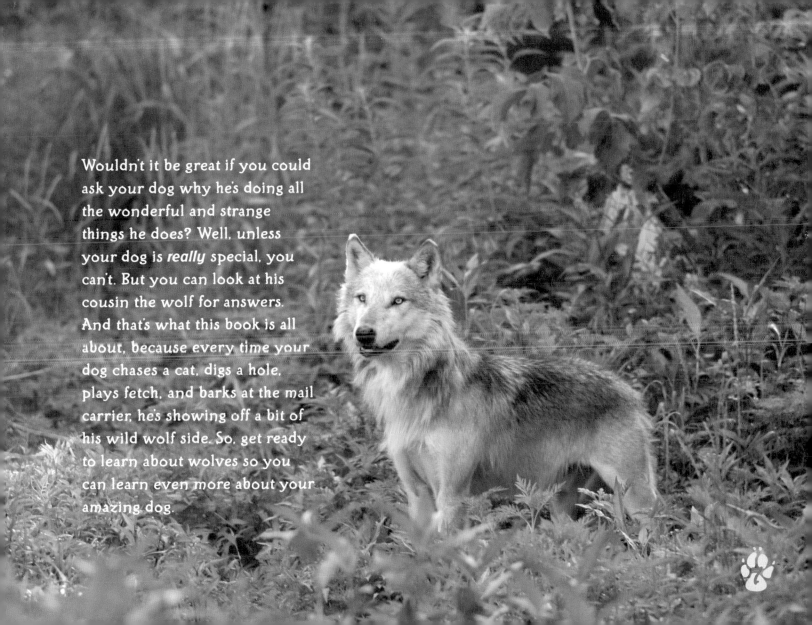

Wouldn't it be great if you could ask your dog why he's doing all the wonderful and strange things he does? Well, unless your dog is *really* special, you can't. But you can look at his cousin the wolf for answers. And that's what this book is all about, because every time your dog chases a cat, digs a hole, plays fetch, and barks at the mail carrier, he's showing off a bit of his wild wolf side. So, get ready to learn about wolves so you can learn even more about your amazing dog.

Close Cousins

Some of your dog's behavior can be explained by studying wolves.

I n the days of your great-great-(add about 1,000 greats)-grandparents, wolves and dogs shared the same ancestor—the ancient wolf. Gradually, over the centuries, dogs evolved and changed to become their own species, and wolves stayed wolves.

8

Even though it has been thousands of years since dogs have been wild, many things a dog does by instinct a wolf also does.

How different are they? Well, you can't tame a wolf and turn it into a dog. And a dog that gets lost in the woods will not become a wolf simply because it doesn't live in someone's home. The two species have changed too much in the past thousands of years.

Once you understand that dogs and wolves are different, you can look at the ways they are similar. For example, a dog shares a lot more characteristics with a wolf than he does with a cat or a person.

Wild Is WILD

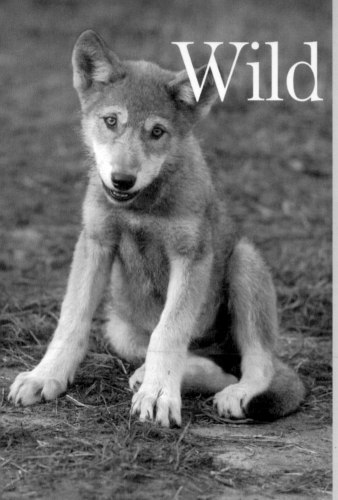

This young wolf might look like a cute puppy, but he's still a wild animal.

Wolves that must spend their lives in zoos or captive areas are often handled by people when they are puppies. As a result, they are more comfortable around humans. This makes it easier to care for captive wolves when they need medicine or when their living area must be cleaned.

However, even hand-raised wolves are quite dangerous. They can seem tame at times, but any good wolf handler knows they're still wild. The wolves that hurt their handlers, animals, or other wolves aren't being mean; they're just being wolves.

Brett was hand-raised at a wolf center and was about as tame as a wolf can become. But when his pack changed and he became the leader, he was suddenly all wolf again.

Workers who had been able to pet him, groom him, and play with him could no longer safely approach him.

You'll probably never see a circus wolf, because they can't be trained as easily as dogs.

Can Wolves Be Trained?

Wolves are very smart animals, but because they are wild, they have much less interest in being trained. They cannot easily (or as reliably) be taught to do tricks, walk on a leash, or sit on command.

Dogs, on the other hand, can be trained to do all sorts of things, from shaking hands and jumping through hoops, to guiding blind people, tracking criminals, and sniffing out illegal drugs.

Newfoundland dogs have historically worked as lifeguards, jumping into the water to help shipwrecked sailors to shore.

Bloodhounds have a keen sense of smell and have been used to track criminals since the Middle Ages.

13

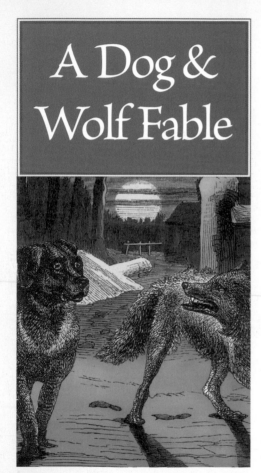

A Dog & Wolf Fable

This fable from Aesop illustrates the difference between dogs and wolves.

A well-fed dog and a hungry wolf met one night. The wolf said, "Why are you so well fed, while I barely have enough to eat?"

"My people feed me," replied the dog. "I only have to guard their house, and they give me lots of crunchy biscuits."

The wolf thought about it, and it seemed like a good deal. He'd get a warm place to sleep and all the food he could want. He decided he would like to be a dog too, and so he started to follow his new friend home.

All at once, the moonlight shimmered on a bit of metal around the dog's neck. Having never seen such a thing, the wolf asked what it was. "Well, it's a collar, of course," said the dog. "It has my name on it so all will know who owns me. And it has a buckle so a leash can be attached to it to keep me close."

In horror, the wolf turned around and headed back to the forest. "Good night my friend, I'll go my own way. I'd rather have my hunger than a collar around my neck."

And that's what separates dogs from wolves. Dogs are happy to live in our homes, while the wolves are happy only in the wild, far from humans.

The black German shepherd puppy and the wolf puppies look to be getting along, but once grown, they would not be friends. In the wild, the wolves would attack the dog.

The Big Bad Wolf?

What do you think of when you imagine a wolf? A scary wild dog?
The Big Bad Wolf that tried to kill Red Riding Hood or wreck the homes of the Three
Little Pigs? An almost mystical animal howling at the moon? Or maybe a werewolf?

These are very exciting ideas about wolves. But none of them is true. Wolves are neither good nor bad. They're just wolves.

Wolves are great hunters, which makes them an important part of the wildlife community. They kill and eat animals much larger than themselves, and they fight fiercely to protect their food and living area from stranger wolves, coyotes, and other animals. Some of these traits can make them seem scary or bad.

Wolves can be found in many countries around the world, but they are in danger everywhere. This is because there are fewer safe places for them to live, less wildlife to eat, and more people trying to kill them.

China, Croatia, Finland, India, Israel, Italy, Poland, and the United States are among the countries creating laws to protect them. Wolves have even been reintroduced to some parts of the United States, including Yellowstone National Park.

Wolves are neither good nor bad. They're just wolves.

17

Wolves &

Coyote

Red Fox

Fennec

Their Relatives

Wolves and dogs are different species of animals. (A species is a group of similar organisms that are considered to be the same kind.) But, since they share many physical traits, scientists list them together in a group of animals called the Canid family. Foxes, coyotes, jackals, and the funny-looking fennec are also in this Canid group.

There are three recognized species of wolves in the world—the gray wolf, red wolf, and Ethiopian (Abyssinian) wolf. Some scientists disagree and think the red wolf is really a type of coyote and that the Ethiopian is a type of jackal. Either way, there are far more gray wolves than any other type.

Around the world, the gray wolf has many subspecies, including Arctic, timber, Mexican, European, Caucasian, Tibetan, and Indian wolves.

Unfortunately, the name "gray wolf" is very misleading, because gray wolves can range in color from white to black. Many are grayish with bits of brown or red. Puppies usually have grayish coats, too.

all Shapes & Sizes

Dogs come in many different sizes, shapes, and colors. Some dogs have solid colors, while others have different-colored markings, spots, or even stripes.

In the last few centuries, people have created hundreds of dog breeds, such as Labrador retrievers, German shepherds, and Chihuahuas. Different dog breeds and mixed breeds (mutts) have different traits and capabilities, which make them better or worse at different tasks.

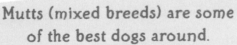

Mutts (mixed breeds) are some
of the best dogs around.

Today, the most important "job" for most dogs is being a well-behaved member of your family (see page 60). But not so long ago, few dogs were pets. Most had important work to do, such as helping people herd livestock, hunt game, guard homes and businesses, or pull sleds and carts.

Having a pure-bred Maltese means your dog will look a lot like other Malteses.

21

Wolf & Dog Packs

Most wolves live in a family structure called a pack, with two parents, their puppies, and a few other adults. Most of these adults are brothers and sisters that are a year or two older, although some may be aunts and uncles, or even unrelated. All the adults in a pack help feed and protect the puppies.

Wolf packs are similar to human families in some ways. In both people families and wolf families, the parents make and enforce the rules.

"Teenage" wolves and other adult wolves help enforce the rules. Teenagers get to do more things than the puppies, such as go on hunts. But they also have more responsibilities, such as helping to care for their younger siblings.

In the **Dog House**

Like wolves, dogs are pack animals that want to live in a group. A pet dog considers his pack to be the humans (and other pets) in his home. Dogs are social creatures, and they don't like being left alone. Most of them need to have friends and family around to feel happy and safe. This is why many dogs do "bad" things when they are left alone. Boredom and fear often lead to destructive behavior, such as chewing the couch, scratching the door, or barking nonstop.

Being alone can be very upsetting to a puppy. Even when they grow up, they'd still rather be with you!

Dogs view the people and other pets in their home as part of their pack.

25

The Nose Knows

Dogs and wolves can see, of course, but their sense of smell is much more important to them. Their sense of smell is thousands of times better than ours. So, it's not surprising that they use their noses more than we do.

26

Think of your room. Picture your bed, desk, clothes, toys, and posters. Humans are very visual. When we think of something, we tend to picture it in our mind.

Your dog probably pictures your room by its smells as well. The smell of your shampoo on your pillow. The stink of your socks under the bed. Sounds crazy, but it's true.

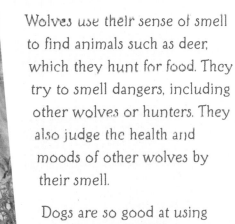

Wolves use their sense of smell to find animals such as deer, which they hunt for food. They try to smell dangers, including other wolves or hunters. They also judge the health and moods of other wolves by their smell.

Dogs are so good at using their noses that many are given smelling jobs. Police dogs use their noses to detect illegal drugs and chase down criminals. The beagle on page 42 sniffs out things hidden in suitcases at airports.

Look at this happy dog. It's a good thing this is not a scratch-and-sniff book, because he loves to find the grossest, stinkiest thing he can and then roll in it!

Experts think wolves and dogs do this to mark this wonderful prize with their own scent, as a way to claim it as their own. Getting all stinky in the process is just an added bonus.

Hear This

Both dogs and wolves can hear better than we can. They can detect quieter noises as well as a wider range of musical notes. That's why we can't hear a high-pitched silent dog whistle, but dogs and wolves can.

All wolves have upright pointy ears, but dogs have a variety of ear shapes. It doesn't seem to matter whether your dog has pointed ears, floppy ears, or tiny ears—they can all hear better than we can.

Wolf and dog ears also do more than just hear. Their shape and position can change, which is an important tool for communication.

Happy

Worried

Perky ears mean they are paying attention to someone or something. Scrunched-up ears, especially on dogs with floppy ears, can mean they're worried or fearful. Flattened ears usually mean a warning or aggression. However, softly flattened ears can also be a friendly sign when the dog is trying to please his leader— you!

Watch your dog's ears so you can learn this important part of dog language.

Through Their Eyes

Golden Retriever   Shar-Pei   Gray Wolf

Dogs and wolves don't see colors as well as most people do. They have trouble telling the difference between red, orange, green, and yellow. This means a yellow toy on a red rug might almost be invisible to them.

Remember, too, that your dog is shorter than you. Pearl (below) is a small dog, no bigger than the average cat. She sees the world from just a few inches off the ground. Try crawling on the floor for a while, and take a look at the world from her height. Everything looks a lot different.

Don't feel too bad for them. They might not be able to appreciate the colors in your art project, but they are excellent at detecting the slightest motion—an important hunting skill.

Some dogs have better eyesight than others. Certain dogs (especially those with long noses, such as greyhounds) prefer to hunt with their eyes rather than with their noses. They're probably using both, but some dogs favor one over the other.

Your dog doesn't need to hunt for its food, but he still has the same hunting tools as wolves.

What Big Teeth You Have!

Wolves have sharp teeth, strong jaws, and thick neck muscles to kill deer, antelope, musk oxen, and other animals for food. When their hunt is successful, they use their teeth to tear through thick hide to get to the meat.

Your dog doesn't need to hunt for his food, unless finding the biscuit jar counts as hunting! But dogs have the same hunting tools as wolves. In fact, some dogs can bite as hard or even harder than wolves can.

Don't be fooled into thinking that just because a dog is little or cute, he's not dangerous. All dogs, regardless of size, need to be trained so they learn that biting is not allowed.

Play Fighting

Scary fight? Nope. These wolves are just having fun, making noise, and play fighting.

Both dogs and wolves like to play fight. It's actually more of a dance than a fight, because there is a lot of noise and action, but rarely does anyone get hurt.

Play fighting helps the wolves keep their hunting and fighting skills in tip-top shape, it relieves tension, and it's a whole lot of fun.

Wolf and dog puppies play fight to learn social skills. If they bite their siblings too hard, then nobody will want to play with them. They quickly learn how to play fight without causing pain or damage.

Dogs need to learn that people can't play fight the same way other dogs can. What seems like a gentle nip to a puppy can draw blood on us. Puppies must be taught that they need to be gentle with people.

The Hunters

Wolves eat a lot of different things, but they prefer eating big game animals, such as deer, elk, bison, and musk oxen. When hunting is poor, they will go for raccoons, rabbits and other smaller animals. Mice, moles, and squirrels make a tasty one-bite snack. Wolves will occasionally eat eggs, fruits, and berries if they find them, but the bulk of their meal is meat.

Once in a while, wolves that live near farms and ranches will kill cattle or horses, because these aren't so different from wolves' natural food. Scientists spend a lot of time trying to figure out how to prevent this. Luckily, most wild wolves avoid people, farms, and ranches.

Even though your pet dog doesn't need to hunt for his dinner, he may enjoy a fun game of "chase me."

Your dog doesn't need to hunt for his dinner, because you pour kibble out of a bag or open up a can of wet dog food. But the instinct is still there. This explains why many dogs love to chase small animals.

It also explains why "chase me" is a great game for dogs to play together. It's okay to play chase with your own dog, because he knows the rules—no hurting people. However, you should never run or move quickly near a dog you don't know, since it could spark that ancient hunting instinct, with you as the target.

Food
Fight

Eating is a matter of life and death for a wolf. Fighting at the dinner table for a share of the kill is part of surviving in the wild. Wolves need to fight to protect their precious food from others, including members of their pack.

Most dogs consider food to be VERY important, and this can make dinnertime stressful for them. They may worry that, like wolves, they need to fight to protect their food from others. If you have more than one dog, feeding them in separate rooms may help.

Many dogs like to eat poop (scientists call it *scat*)—goose and rabbit droppings, cow patties, horse manure, and even their own poop.

Wolves do it because there is some nutritional value in it. But there's no reason for your dog, who probably licks your face, to do it. Clean up after your dog so that he doesn't learn this yucky habit.

Fat Dogs

There is no such thing as a fat wolf in the wild, because wolves hunt only for what they need. But most people overfeed their dogs, and don't realize they are getting fat.

Many dogs will overeat if given the chance. They seem so happy when you give them treats that it's hard to resist. Dogs are very clever beggars and quickly learn that cute expressions or tricks win them biscuits. Don't be tempted to give them a treat if they ask you by barking or scratching—it will just teach them that this annoying behavior works.

After all, has your mother ever let you eat five desserts because you're starving? I bet not.

It's important that you keep your dog trim and fit, because fat dogs can become sick or crippled, and may not live as long.

Howling & YOWLING

Wolves love to howl, which is best described as wolf singing. Howling together seems to be a bonding experience for the whole wolf family. A few types of dogs, such as beagles and bloodhounds, love to howl as well.

Wolves usually bark only as a warning about possible intruders. But barking is probably the most common dog noise. In fact, dogs tend to bark **a lot**. They bark to warn you about strangers. They bark when they play. They bark when they want attention. And some bark just because they're bored.

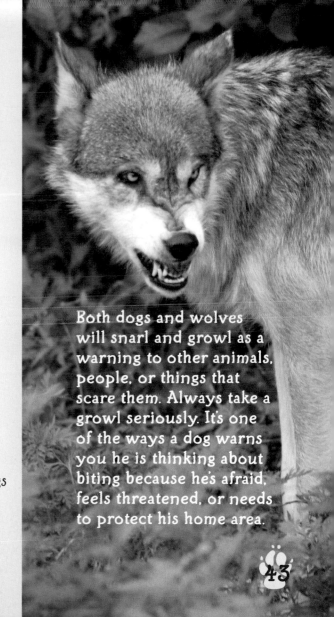

Both dogs and wolves will snarl and growl as a warning to other animals, people, or things that scare them. Always take a growl seriously. It's one of the ways a dog warns you he is thinking about biting because he's afraid, feels threatened, or needs to protect his home area.

Secret Wolf Codes

Every kid knows that dogs speak with barks instead of words—but did you know they speak with body language as well? Both dogs and wolves share this same language. You'll get a chance to see this behavior on the next several pages. Once you learn these secret wolf codes, you may be surprised by what your dog is saying.

Gray Wolf

Bow Wow Wow

The puppy on the left thinks he just met a new friend in the mirror. He's bowing to invite him to play.

When a dog bows down on his front legs (with his bottom in the air), it's usually an invitation for you or another dog to come play.

A Cautionary Tail!

Watch out for a dog that looks like the wolf at the bottom. His tucked tail, arched back, and low head tell you he is afraid. If you see a dog acting like this, let him leave. Don't follow him. He's trying to get away, and by following, you might make him think you are trying to chase or corner him. He might bite you out of fear.

Roll Over Rover

Rolling on his back is one way a young wolf or dog says, "I know you're the boss." When playing, it's like saying, "Uncle! I give up!"

Tales of the Tail

If your dog has a long tail, he probably does a lot of talking with it. Happy wagging is easy to read on most dogs (and wolves). A tucked tail means a dog or wolf is scared or worried. A stiff tail means that a dog or wolf is ready to fight.

Heads or Tails?

The white wolf at right is the boss of the gray colored one. Putting her head over his shoulders is one way to tell him this. He understands, and answers by tucking his tail, arching his back, and softly tucking his ears back.

Dogs do this, too. In the second photo on the right, the German shepherd is putting his head over the other dog. He has his tail lifted high and is walking tall and very stiff. He is announcing that he is boss. The other dog agrees.

Why Does My Dog's Hair STAND UP?

Raised hair on the back and neck of a dog or wolf (called *hackles*) is a warning that he's ready to fight (because he is either really tough or really scared). Showing his teeth is an even more forceful statement. If a dog does either or both of these things near you, look away from the dog, don't move, and wait for an adult to help. Never run.

When an adult wolf growls at a puppy but doesn't have raised hackles (right), it is usually just a scolding, rather than the start of a fight.

staring
Contest

How your dog looks at you can tell you a lot. There is a big difference between a hard aggressive stare and a soft, "smiley" glance. Your dog probably looks at you in a friendly way when he wants a biscuit or is waiting for a command. However, if a dog that you don't know starts staring intensely at you, he could be challenging you. Pick a friendlier dog to play with.

Love to Lick My Face?

Ready to be grossed out? He could be asking you to vomit! Once wolf puppies start weaning off their mother's milk, all the adult wolves in the pack help feed them by vomiting their meals for the pups to eat. It's not a very delicious-sounding meal to us, but it's an important part of a wolf puppy's diet.

As they get older, some wolves will lick the face of another wolf to show respect or to try to avoid punishment by appearing more puppy-like (and therefore less threatening).

Dogs are no different from wolves in this respect. Puppies lick the faces of adult dogs and people. But, because we supply them with ample puppy food, they're probably not hungry. They're just recognizing us as the boss.

Why Does My Dog Chew My Stuff?

It's not because he's mad at you.

The wolf pup below is chewing on a deer antler for several reasons. There is some small nutritional value gained by chewing antlers and crunching on bones. It is also the way wolves brush their teeth. (The rough texture of bones scrapes the teeth clean.) But mostly, it is just fun and tastes good.

Most of us don't leave antlers lying around the house, so table legs, shoes, and hockey sticks probably seem like good antler substitutes.

Many dogs get scared or bored when they are left alone, and chewing on something can be comforting and entertaining to them. If that "something" smells like you, it is all the more appealing. So when he eats your homework, it really means he misses having you around—but don't try explaining that to your teacher.

This dog chews on sticks in the yard. So when he found a really cool "stick" in the living room, he couldn't understand why he was scolded.

What's So Great about Squeaky Toys?

You might enjoy board games, computer games, action figures, or dolls, but it's kind of hard to figure out why so many dogs go crazy over squeaky toys—until you think about wolves.

When wolves hunt, they target the weakest animals, such as the old, young, injured, or sick. This might seem unfair, but it is actually a very important part of the natural world. By eating the weakest deer, for example, the wolves help make sure the strongest and healthiest survive and become parents.

A squeaky toy sounds a lot like an injured animal, so it may trigger the wolf-like hunting instincts in your dog. Many dogs even rip apart their stuffed toys, like a wolf would a rabbit or bird.

Some dogs also love to shake their heads back and forth when playing with their toys. If those toys were rabbits or birds, this shaking would break their necks and kill them. Your dog may never have gone hunting, but he still has this ancient instinct.

Dogs such as golden retrievers and Labrador retrievers are usually really good at playing fetch. That's because, over many generations, bird hunters have chosen dogs that were willing to run and retrieve a dead bird after it had been shot. Today, bringing back a tennis ball must seem a lot like bringing back a bird.

Why Does My Dog

Grab My Stuff?

Dogs love to play tug-of-war. It's a play version of another important wolf survival skill. When hunting, the ability to grab hold and pull helps wolves bring down a big animal.

Once that animal is killed, tug-of-war skills help tear off large pieces of meat from the bone so wolves can eat as quickly as possible, before other wolves and animals can get to it. Later, tugging skills help wolves drag remaining pieces of meat to safe hiding places.

Tug-of-war may be a fun game to play with your dog, but you'll need to set up some rules. Your dog should never be allowed to grab the toy from your hand, because you could get bitten in all the excitement. Instead, offer the toy to the dog with a command such as "gentle." If he is not gentle when he takes the toy, drop it and walk away. Your dog will soon learn that the fun ends if he gets grabby.

Tug-of-war is a wolf hunting game.

Why Does My Dog Dig?

Digging is a survival tool for wolves, but it's just plain old fun for dogs.

This wolf puppy is burying a bone.

Wolves dig holes to hide leftover food and bones, so they'll have a nice snack for later. Some dig to catch small underground animals such as mice and moles, which make tasty snacks. Or they dig to create a cool hole to lie in during the summer (lower left) or a warm snow cave in the winter. Adult wolves dig underground dens for puppies to provide shelter and safety.

Dogs may dig for some of the same reasons, but one thing is for sure: freshly dug dirt has all sorts of interesting smells. And dogs (and wolves) love to use their noses.

59

In the wild, wolves live by wolf rules. Most of their days are spent caring for the young, resting, and hunting. Dogs, however, must live by people rules both inside and outside the home. Their willingness to do this is probably the biggest difference between the two species.

People rules vary from household to household, but almost always they mean no snacks from the garbage can, no chewing on furniture or eating homework, no nipping fingers when given a biscuit, no jumping out of the tub before bathtime is done, and no driving the family go-cart.

Dogs are willing to learn all kinds of human rules.

Where to Meet Wolves

This book shows you many of the ways that dogs and wolves are similar and different. Certain ancient instincts make them act the same. But, unlike wolves, dogs have unique traits that make them good family members.

It's easy to observe your dog and your friends' dogs. Learning about wolves is a little harder. Wolves usually try to avoid humans, so it's doubtful you'll ever see one in his natural environment. This is a good thing, because we don't want wolves approaching people. The quickest way to create a dangerous wild wolf is to take away his fear of people by feeding him, or just by leaving an unclean campsite where he can find food.

Visit a zoo or wildlife center, or go to an approved viewing area in a national park to see wolves. The wolves in this book were photographed at the Wildlife Science Center in Forest Lake, Minnesota. Visit **www.wildlifesciencecenter.org** to learn more about these and other wolves.

Wolves have successfully been reintroduced to Yellowstone National Park. Log onto **www.nps.gov/yell** to find out more about the wolf packs that live there, or visit your local zoo or nature center to learn more about wolf-viewing opportunities in your area.

Now that you know more about dogs and wolves, the real fun begins. It's time to run and play, and *watch* your dog. So get outside and explore your wild sides!

Photo Credits

All photos by Jenni Bidner, except as noted below.

AtWag: Page 18 (middle photo)

Eric Bean: Page 33 (right photo), page 45 (photo of puppy in mirror), and page 61 (bottom photo)

Andrea von Buddenbrock: Page 40 (right photo) and page 55 (right photo)

Corbis: Page 18 (right photo)

Cheryl Croston: Page 21 (right photo)

Greg Friese: Page 59 (right photos)

Louis Agassiz Fuertes: Page 20 (illustration)

Anne Gridley Grave: Page 25 (photo of puppy at door)

Lanica Klein: Page 18 (left photo)

Ellen Labenski: Page 31

Jessie Wilcox Smith: Page 16 (illustration)

Nancy Thornton: Page 12 (main photo), page 47 (top right photo), and page 55 (left photo)

Meleda Wegner: Page 8 (left photo) and page 39 (left photo)

Index

64